THE JAMES THRALL SOBY COLLECTION

of works of art pledged or given to The Museum of Modern Art

cover: Shahn, see page 64

frontispiece: Picasso, see page 62

exhibited for the benefit of the Museum's Library

at M. Knoedler and Company, Inc., 14 East 57 Street,

New York, February 1 to February 25, 1961, as a

contribution to the Museum's 30th Anniversary Fund

THE MUSEUM OF MODERN ART, NEW YORK

distributed by Doubleday & Company, Inc., Garden City, New York

This exhibition is dedicated to a person, a cause and a hope. The person is my wife, Melissa. The cause is the Museum of Modern Art's Library, on whose staff and resources I have depended for many years in matters of research. The hope is that these works of art, all of them bequeathed or already given to the Museum, will find space on the walls of the new Museum of Modern Art.

J. T. S.

GIORGIO DE CHIRICO. Italian, born Greece 1888.
The Seer. 1915. Oil on canvas, 35¼ x 27⅜". Acquired
1940.

"*The Seer* as an image is the very epitome of the dire,
even if warmed by an incalculable poetry of nostalgic
mood. Its central figure is depicted as a motionless, brood-
ing presence, perched with wing-like shoulders on a ped-
estal and facing a blackboard on which appear an architectural drawing, some cryptic letters, the word 'Torino'
and the outline of a statue. This is the work of an artist
convinced of the power of oracles, as we know from first-
hand evidence de Chirico actually was in youth.

"The setting of *The Seer* appears to be an exterior
court or square, bounded in the distance by a toy-like
building which Alfred H. Barr, Jr. has suggested to the
writer may have been inspired by one of the many small,
'portable' buildings in Giotto's frescoes. (The suggestion
seems pertinent in that de Chirico would certainly have
seen Giotto's works in the Church of Santa Croce at Flor-
ence.) But the ground before the building is covered with
wooden planking, as in *The Duo* (page 33) and *The
Double Dream of Spring* (page 36). This fact implies
that the scene takes place indoors. Remembering de Chirico's love of enigmas, it may well be that he used the
flooring to convey a sense of uncertainty, sometimes felt
in late pictures in the Caravaggesque tradition, as to
whether a given action occurs within a chamber or in the
open air.

"The superb mannequin figure dominates *The Seer*
through its eloquent strength of contour. . . . Its white
head is astonishingly luminous, picking up a greenish re-
flection from the sky at the left and building up to a
blinding white in the center, its foil the intense black of
the image on the easel which is held aloft by those strange
armatures which were soon to play so important a part in
the painter's iconography."—adapted from (17) *Giorgio
de Chirico*

6

PREFACE

It is with the greatest sense of pride and satisfaction that the Museum of Modern Art presents to the New York public this exhibition of painting and sculpture from the collection of James Thrall Soby. Every work of art in the exhibition has been pledged by Mr. Soby to this Museum, and a number are already in its possession. This act of generosity on the part of Mr. Soby and his family is a characteristic example of his devoted interest in our institution. We believe that you will recognize as you visit the galleries the distinction and high quality of the collection and will appreciate the Museum's good fortune in being the eventual recipient of these fine works. The proceeds derived from the benefit exhibition will go, at Mr. Soby's request, to the Museum's 30th Anniversary Building and Endowment Fund specifically in connection with the modernization and expansion of the Museum's Library.

Mr. Soby has been a Trustee of the Museum of Modern Art since 1942 and has served the institution in various other important capacities. He was Director of the Armed Services Program from 1942 to 1945 and Director of Painting and Sculpture as well as Assistant Director of the Museum from 1943 to 1945. He has been Chairman of the Department of Painting and Sculpture Exhibitions from 1946 to the present time and has carried for fifteen years the important responsibility of the Chairmanship of the Trustees' Committee on the Museum Collections. In the performance of these duties he has combined most successfully the points of view of a highly knowledgeable and scholarly professional with the more personal touch of a private collector and patron of the arts. He is a man greatly loved and respected by his associates, both lay and professional.

The important exhibitions which Mr. Soby has himself directed for the Museum since 1941 number fourteen in all, including many one-man shows and such comprehensive reviews as the painting section of the Museum's Fifteenth Anniversary Exhibition held in 1944, and the more recent large "Twentieth Century Italian Art from American Collections" just back from showing this past summer in Milan and Rome under the auspices of the Museum's International Council. Mr. Soby has a distinguished reputation as a scholar and critic in the field of contemporary art and has to his great credit over twenty monographs and collections of essays. His contribution to the Museum of Modern Art's publications program has been of capital importance.

It is because of Mr. Soby's frequent use of the Museum Library's services in the preparation of these many exhibitions and publications that he wishes to emphasize the particular importance of this department and its present needs. He speaks of this interest in the statement immediately following this preface. The Board of Trustees and the 30th Anniversary Committee are fully in accord with the emphasis which this benefit puts on the Library's urgently needed share in our expansion program. To function effectively, the Library must have more funds so that it can adequately house its unsurpassed collection of books, periodicals, catalogues, clippings and photographs on the modern arts. The Library must be able to organize this material with modernized equipment, up-to-date techniques and additional staff so that it may serve research scholars, students, collectors and the growing non-specialized public. Once this is achieved the Library and its archives, together with the Collections, will be the core of the Museum's international center for study and research, a function to which it brings at present unique resources but woefully inadequate facilities.

The 30th Anniversary Building and Endowment Drive of the Museum of Modern Art is a major effort on the part of its Trustees to secure more exhibition space for the Museum's collections, more offices and working facilities for its overcrowded and overburdened staff, and more permanent security for the Museum's total program through much needed capital endowment. The Museum has been fortunate in the notable success it has achieved in its first thirty years. It has had many kind and generous benefactors who have contributed their works of art and their annual gifts to the institution. But now it cannot carry out its obligations to these benefactors and to the public without expanding its total facilities and exhibition galleries.

It is the hope of the Board of Trustees that this benefit exhibition will serve to emphasize to all who visit it two of the Museum's greatest needs. We must have a better, more spacious and more usable library suitable for an institution which has already come to be looked upon as an international study center for the arts of our time. Further, we urgently require more gallery space to show to our members and the general public a higher proportion of our unparalleled permanent collection. The masterpieces in Mr. Soby's magnificent gift to the collection must be on view in future years for the benefit and enjoyment of the Museum's many visitors.

This preface would not be complete without speaking of the kind generosity and assistance of the many good friends of the Museum of Modern Art who have made this benefit exhibition possible. The Museum's Officers and Trustees wish to express, first and foremost, their great appreciation to Mr. Soby for having loaned his collection for public showing at this particularly appropriate point in our fund-raising. We are grateful also to the members of the Benefit Committee and to its Chairman, Mrs. C. Sterling Bunnell, and to her four Vice-Chairmen, Mrs. Ethan A. Hitchcock, Mrs. Victor W. Ganz, Mrs. Samuel Taylor and Mrs. Donald B. Straus. All of these ladies have worked hard to make the event an outstanding success.

To M. Knoedler & Company and particularly to its officers, Mr. Roland Balay and Mr. E. Coe Kerr, Jr., are due our warm thanks for making their galleries and the services of their firm available to the Museum for this occasion. Miss Jane Sabersky of Knoedler and Miss Betsy Jones of the Museum Staff have been particularly helpful in preparing the exhibition and the catalogue.

Finally, Mr. Alfred H. Barr, Jr., Director of the Museum Collections, has been responsible for the over-all selection of the works of art. A warm friend and admirer of Mr. Soby, Alfred Barr has worked in the closest cooperation and harmony with him to make this a memorable exhibition.

To both of these men, and to everyone who has had a part, either large or small, in the preparation of this benefit we wish to offer heartfelt thanks.

BLANCHETTE H. ROCKEFELLER, *President*

The following list does not include books for which substantial documentation may have been supplied in other forms, and omits, of course, the Museum's own publications for which 63 bibliographies have been prepared.

The letters in parentheses following each entry refer to the compiler of the bibliography. (K) indicates those prepared by Bernard Karpel, the Librarian; those followed by (A) were done by Henry Aronson, (H) by Sylvia Hill, (M) by Hannah Muller, all former members of the Library staff.

Daniel-Henry Kahnweiler. *Juan Gris*. New York, London, 1947 (M)

St. Louis Museum. *Max Beckmann*. 1948 (M)

Jean Arp. *On My Way*. New York, 1948 (K)

Max Ernst. *Beyond Painting*. New York, 1948 (K)

Guillaume Apollinaire. *The Cubist Painters*. New York, 1949 (K)

Daniel-Henry Kahnweiler. *The Rise of Cubism*. New York, 1949 (K)

Douglas Cooper. *Fernand Léger*. Geneva, 1949 (M)

Herbert Read. *Henry Moore*. New York, London, 1949 (M)

Marcel Raymond. *From Baudelaire to Surrealism*. New York, 1950 (K)

Georges Duthuit. *Les Fauves*. Geneva, 1949 (K) Also Swedish edition. Revised American edition: *The Fauvist Painters*, New York, 1950.

Robert Melville. *Graham Sutherland*. London, 1950 (A)

Maurice Raynal (*et al.*). *History of Modern Painting*. Geneva, 1950 (K-M) Also French and German editions.

Kunstsamlingers Arbok. *Edvard Munch, A Bibliography*. Oslo, 1951 (M)

Robert Motherwell & Ad Reinhardt. *Modern Artists in America*. New York, 1951 (K)

Carola Giedion-Welcker. *Paul Klee*. New York, 1952 (M) Also German edition: Stuttgart, 1954.

Katharine Kuh. *Léger*. University of Illinois, 1953 (M)

Will Grohmann. *Paul Klee*. Stuttgart, 1954 (M) Other editions: New York, Geneva.

White Museum. *Arthur G. Dove*. Cornell University, 1954 (M)

Gerd Hatje. *Idea 55: International Design Annual*. New York, Stuttgart, 1955 (K) Also in another tri-lingual edition: *New Furniture*, 1955.

House Beautiful. *Frank Lloyd Wright Number*. New York, 1955 (K). Second *Number* issued 1959.

Carola Giedion-Welcker. *Contemporary Sculpture*. New York, 1955 (K) Also German edition: Stuttgart, 1955.

Will Grohmann. *Schmidt-Rottluff*. Stuttgart, 1956 (K) Also edition with English introduction.

Herbert Read & Leslie Martin. *Gabo*. London, Cambridge, 1957 (K)

Arts Council, London. *S. W. Hayter Retrospective*. 1958 (K)

Charles McCurdy. *Modern Art: a Pictorial Anthology*. New York, 1958 (K)

Sam Hunter. *Modern American Painting & Sculpture*. New York, 1958 (K)

Will Grohmann. *Wassily Kandinsky*. Cologne, 1958 (K) Also American edition: New York, 1958.

Theodore Brenson. *Light into Color*. Rutgers University, 1959 (K)

Hans Hess. *Lyonel Feininger*. Cologne, 1960 (K) New York edition due 1961.

Announced for Publication

Mary Callery. *Sculpture by Callery*. New York, 1961 (K)

Douglas Cooper. *Graham Sutherland*. London, 1961 (K)

James Thrall Soby. *Ben Shahn*. New York, 1961 (H)

In Preparation

Jacques Dupin. *Joan Miró*. (K)

Franz Meyer. *Marc Chagall*. (K)

Bernard Karpel. *Arts of the Twentieth Century: A Bibliography*.

THE MUSEUM'S LIBRARY

The Library of the Museum of Modern Art has brought to that institution a unique and enviable distinction. Established in 1932 through a gift of books from the Museum's first President, General A. Conger Goodyear, the Library has acquired an unrivaled collection of research material in the Museum's special field—the visual arts from roughly 1875 to the present. Its shelves hold over 15,000 books, catalogues and periodicals; its files contain thousands of clippings and documents; its pictorial archives of photographs and slides cover about 100,000 subjects. Of equal importance to the student, critic, museum curator or interested layman has been the extraordinary efficiency and knowledgeableness of the Library's staff, now consisting of the Librarian, Bernard Karpel, and eight assistants. The Museum's bibliographies are held in very high esteem throughout the world; the Librarian himself is respected as one of modern art's most perceptive and diligent bibliographers. The Library's catalogue of lantern slides for sale to teachers and lecturers has set a precedent and a standard.

Apart from professional qualifications, a word must be said about the unfailing helpfulness of the Library's staff. Lacking space and personnel, the Library cannot yet be opened to the general public, but no one truly interested in its resources has been turned from its doors. The Museum's curatorial departments use the Library constantly in preparing exhibitions and publications. And from all over America and Europe people arrive to do research.

It is a mystery how the Library's staff can maintain capable equanimity when faced with so many practical limitations. Having tripled its holdings, the Library has less space today than when the 53rd Street building was opened in 1939. Twenty years ago the Library's funds for books and periodicals were inadequate. Since then they have barely doubled in the face of the enormous increase both in numbers and prices of books on the modern arts. The slides for rent do not begin to fill the needs of lecturers. The Library lacks sufficient catalogue units, slide cabinets, steel files, metal shelving and room for negatives and photographic equipment.

This is a great Library, superbly staffed. It has been made so by the successive Librarians—Iris Barry, Beaumont Newhall and Bernard Karpel, with such able assistants as Hannah Muller and Pearl Moeller. It is handicapped by insufficient funds. The purpose of this exhibition is to raise money for the Library and—perhaps more important—to focus public attention on the Library's past achievements, present needs, and hopes for additional resources to make possible imaginative exploration of new methods of documentation and research.

JAMES THRALL SOBY

In addition to the publications listed below, Mr. Soby has written many other forewords for exhibition catalogues and numerous articles for periodicals including: *The Art Bulletin, Arts Digest, Art in America, Art News, Arts-Spectacles, Cahiers d'Art, The Carnegie Magazine, The College Art Journal, Fashion and Travel, Graphis, Harper's Bazaar, Horizon* (London), *The Ladies' Home Journal, Magazine of Art, Minicam Photography, Parnassus, Perspectives USA, La Revista Belga, Salamander, Studio, Town and Country, Transatlantic, U.S. Camera, View, Vogue.*

From 1946 to 1957 as a Contributing Editor of *The Saturday Review of Literature* he wrote a monthly column of art criticism for that magazine. He was Acting Editor of *Magazine of Art* for 1950–51 and Chairman of its Editorial Board in the years 1951–53.

1 *After Picasso.* Hartford, E. V. Mitchell [and] New York, Dodd, Mead & Co., 1935.

2 *Balthus, Paintings.* New York, Pierre Matisse Gallery, 1938. (Foreword)

3 *Salvador Dali: Paintings, Drawings, Prints.* New York, Museum of Modern Art, 1941 and 1946.

4 *The Early Chirico.* New York, Dodd, Mead & Co., 1941.

5 *Eugene Berman.* Boston, Institute of Modern Art, 1941. (Preface)

6 *Tchelitchew: Paintings, Drawings.* New York, Museum of Modern Art, 1942.

7 *Romantic Painting in America.* New York, Museum of Modern Art, 1943. (With Dorothy C. Miller)

8 *The Prints of Paul Klee.* New York, Curt Valentin, 1945.

9 *Georges Rouault: Paintings and Prints.* New York, Museum of Modern Art, 1945.

10 *Ben Shahn.* West Drayton (England), Penguin Books; New York, Museum of Modern Art, 1947.

11 *Ben Shahn.* Museum of Modern Art Bulletin, Vol. XIV, nos. 4–5, 1947.

12 *Contemporary Painters.* New York, Museum of Modern Art, 1948.

13 *Le Corbusier: Architect, Painter, Writer.* New York, Macmillan Co., 1948. (With Stamo Papadaki, ed., Joseph Hudnut, S. Giedion, F. Léger, J. L. Sert)

14 *Paintings, Drawings and Prints by Paul Klee from the Klee Foundation, Berne, Switzerland, with Additions from American Collections.* New York, Museum of Modern Art, 1949. (Introduction)

15 *Twentieth-Century Italian Art.* New York, Museum of Modern Art, 1949. (With Alfred H. Barr, Jr.)

16 *Modigliani: Paintings, Drawings, Sculpture.* New York, Museum of Modern Art, 1951.

17 *Giorgio de Chirico.* New York, Museum of Modern Art, 1955.

18 *Yves Tanguy.* New York, Museum of Modern Art, 1955.

19 *De David à Toulouse-Lautrec: Chefs-d'oeuvres des collections américaines.* Paris, Musée de l'Orangerie, 1955. (Foreword)

20 *15 Paintings by French Masters of the Nineteenth Century.* New York, Museum of Modern Art, 1955.

21 *Balthus.* New York, Museum of Modern Art, 1956.

22 *New Art in America: Fifty Painters of the 20th Century.* Greenwich, Conn., New York Graphic Society [and] New York, Praeger, 1957. (With John I. H. Baur, ed., Lloyd Goodrich, Dorothy C. Miller and Frederick S. Wight)

23 *Ben Shahn: His Graphic Art.* New York, Braziller, 1957.

24 *Modern Art and the New Past.* Norman, Oklahoma, University of Oklahoma Press, 1957.

25 *Juan Gris.* New York, Museum of Modern Art, 1958.

26 *Arp.* New York, Museum of Modern Art, 1958. (Editing and introduction; articles by Jean Arp, Richard Huelsenbeck, Robert Melville, Carola Giedion-Welcker)

27 *Joan Miró.* New York, Museum of Modern Art, 1959.

28 *Arte Italiana del XX Secolo da Collezioni Americane.* Milan, "Silvana" Editoriale d'Arte, 1960. (Introduction)

29 *Ben Shahn.* New York, Braziller. (To be published in 1961)

30 *Francis Bacon.* New York, Museum of Modern Art. (To be published in 1961)

31 *Ben Shahn.* New York, Harry N. Abrams. (In preparation)

JAMES THRALL SOBY AND HIS COLLECTION

James Thrall Soby has distinguished himself as an eloquent and independent critic, an imaginative scholar of painstaking probity, an able, devoted museum man and a collector of excellent and highly personal taste.

Mr. Soby's museum career began at the Hartford Atheneum where in 1931 he helped organize the first museum exhibition of Surrealism and, three years later, the first major Picasso retrospective in this country. Some of his varied services to the Museum of Modern Art are recalled by our President in her preface. No other trustee has worked for the Museum in so many ways or with greater selflessness. In an institution subject to the strains of such rapid growth, unprecedented responsibilities and unforeseen crises, James Soby has stepped into the breach again and again. Whether serving as a regular member of the staff, as he did for four years, an experienced volunteer or a responsible chairman of committees, his work has been highly professional and, as I can testify better than anyone, carried on with a modesty, a patience, an efficiency and a sense of humor which have won for him both the admiration of his colleagues and their deep affection.

The fairness and breadth of Mr. Soby's art criticism depends not upon a cool eclecticism but upon a capacity to respond with generous sympathy to many kinds of art. He has, it is true, certain prejudices: against dogma, for instance, and the assumption of exclusive virtue by an avant-garde. A dozen years ago, in the preface to his *Contemporary Painters* he wrote: "It seems to me that we pre-empt a function of history when we attempt to decide unreservedly what kinds of art are truly 'modern' and what are static or reactionary. . . . The story of Ingres is a case in point. Considered a fussy obstructionist by the rebels of his day, he has been hailed as a revolutionary, along with Cézanne and Seurat, by such pioneers of contemporary art as the cubists and purists . . . even from an advanced viewpoint, the romantic-realist Hopper is as valid a subject for study as Soutine the expressionist. And I speak not only of intrinsic quality, but of possible meaning for later generations of painters. We are not going to settle in our time the direction art *must* take; now, as always, good painters will follow divergent paths to conflicting yet equally rewarding goals." The essays which follow, written for the most part in 1947, include dialectical comparisons between such opposites as Max Weber and Edward Hopper, Ben Shahn and Morris Graves, de Chirico and Boccioni. There are also discerning paragraphs on Pollock and other young painters who at that time were just beginning to be called Abstract Expressionists. (Several years earlier, in 1944, Mr. Soby had been the responsible curator when the Museum bought its first Pollock.)

Unlike critics who prudently avoid personal contacts with artists, Jim Soby has risked bias and occasional disenchantment by forming warm friendships with a large number of artists over the past three decades. In recent years his cottage at Southampton, the summer capital of the "New York School," has made it possible for him to get to know many of the leaders of post-war American painting in an atmosphere of leisurely informality. Mr. Soby believes, and I agree wholeheartedly, that the ideas of artists, in spite of natural bias and egoism, are of great importance to the critic.

MIRÓ. *Still Life with Old Shoe.* (See page 56)

Just as a strong sense of history has given his criticism perspective, Mr. Soby's scholarship has been enriched by his broad experience as critic, editor and museum man. In these roles he has helped to make history, so that in much of his historical writing one feels the latent authority of participation or, at least, first-hand observation. His most important book and in my opinion the best monograph on a living artist, the *Giorgio de Chirico*, is admirable not only for its scrupulous and imaginative research but also for the discerning analyses of the paintings themselves. In writing this book, Mr. Soby had a rare advantage—he could walk out of his study and see the finest collection of de Chiricos in the world.

Whatever the importance of the first impression, or however often one may return to study a master's work on museum walls, there is no substitute for the intimate, revealing, day-to-day living with a picture in coming to understand and appraise it. Mr. Soby's criticism has been refined, strengthened and deepened by his collection.

Mr. Soby himself has very recently written for *Art in America* a candid and highly entertaining account of his collecting since 1925 when as a college sophomore he bought a reproduction of a print by Maxfield Parrish—"a nude but sensibly misty young girl perched on a swing over an arcadian terrace." Five years later he acquired a Matisse and by 1933 owned several more Matisses, four Derains and two Picassos. These painters were the established "big three" in those days, so that the young collector was exhibiting conventional good taste. Eventually he let all his paintings by the two French masters go. Three of these he regrets; he kept an exquisite small Bonnard still life.

Even in these first years Mr. Soby was guilty of certain lapses from established canons. In 1930 he was much taken with the *Portrait of Mrs. Mills in 1750* shown in Miró's first New York show and would have bought it had not the stubborn owner refused to sell until thirteen years later (page 57). His first Picasso was the charming, meditative *The Sigh* (page 63), but in the following year he bought the *Seated Woman*, an icon of radical and uncompromising power (frontispiece). These two Picassos, acquired when the collector was not

yet thirty, and never relinquished, suggest a taste bold enough to confront the formidable, yet broad enough to honor the gentle.

While he was buying the Picassos, the Derains, and the Matisses, Mr. Soby grew interested in two movements which had been initiated in Paris during the previous decade. The Neo-Romantics were retrospective, their works minor in key, overt in melancholy sentiment. The Surrealists were romantic, too, but in the most violent, reckless and subversive sense of the word. Both movements were opposed in principle to the esthetics of abstract art, both accepted, indeed cultivated, poetic associations, and both often used traditional, representational techniques in their paintings. The Neo-Romantics were influenced by Picasso's early pictures of the Blue and Circus periods and would have admired *The Sigh*. In their pursuit of the marvelous, the Surrealists enthusiastically revalued Picasso's cubism, not as form but as fantasy, and, chiefly through the poets, Breton and Eluard, they drew the great painter close to their movement, acclaiming the Surrealist virtues of such works as his *Seated Woman* of 1927. In 1935 Mr. Soby published the first American book on Surrealism and Neo-Romanticism. He called it *After Picasso*.

Looking back twenty-five years later, Neo-Romanticism as a movement seems minor; but, as individuals, two of its major figures, Eugene Berman and his brother Léonid, are still active and honored; Tchelitchew and Bérard have both died since the Second War. All four are admirably represented in Mr. Soby's collection, chiefly by paintings of the 1930's.

By those artists closely associated with Surrealism, Mr. Soby owns excellent paintings by Miró, Tanguy, Dali and Matta, minor works by Ernst, Arp and Masson, a fine post-Surrealist figure by Giacometti, and the great Picasso *Seated Woman*, not to mention photographs by Man Ray and the most famous of Joseph Cornell's objects, now in the Museum of Modern Art. Many of these Mr. Soby has examined in his notes published on the following pages. But I should like to call special attention here to two works by Miró because of their unique character and extraordinary quality. To my mind, the *Self Portrait* (page 59) and the *Still Life with Old Shoe* (page 17) reveal more than anything else the special and courageous vision of James Soby as a collector.

Perhaps I should qualify this superlative in the face of Mr. Soby's incomparable group of eight canvases by de Chirico, the master who so greatly influenced both the Neo-Romantics and the Surrealists, surpassing the former in his evocation of mystery and melancholy, and the latter by the intensity of his hallucinatory, anti-rational imagery. Two enviable paintings represent another great precursor of Surrealism, Paul Klee, to whom the collector has paid frequent homage in his writings.

Among other artists who have worked in the romantic or Surrealist spirit should be mentioned Francis Bacon (about whom Mr. Soby is writing his next book), Balthus with his early masterpiece, *The Street* (page 25), Kay Sage Tanguy, Loren MacIver, Peter Blume, Graham Sutherland, Jean Dubuffet and, youngest of all, Jasper Johns. Grace Hartigan's big *Shinnecock Canal* (page 46) is abstract expressionist in style but with Mr. Soby's guidance a Long Island landscape may be deciphered.

It could be argued that there is a strain of romanticism in certain paintings by Ben Shahn but it is scarcely visible in the pathos of *Father and Child* (page 64) or in the unsmiling faces of the gyrating children in *Liberation* (reproduced on the cover). No artist, not even de Chirico, owes more to Mr. Soby's critical enthusiasm.

There are no purely abstract paintings in Mr. Soby's collection excepting a watercolor by the sculptor, Sandy Calder, whose mobile relief, *Swizzle Sticks* (page 31) is one of his most memorable works. The sculpture in the collection is admirably selected though with a less idiosyncratic taste than the painting. Of the older works the superb Lehmbruck torso (page 50) is much the most important; Maillol is seen in two small bronzes. The collector was one of the first Americans to buy the work of Marino Marini, whose robust *Dancer* (page 52) stabilizes the Soby lawn in New Canaan which otherwise might succumb to the inconstant motion of Calder's *Well Sweep*, a mobile far too large and lively for indoor exhibition. The recent and flourishing British school of sculpture is well seen in works by Butler and Chadwick. The fine Giacometti, already mentioned, was given the collector on his fiftieth birthday by his wife, Melissa.

Only a few of Mr. Soby's many drawings and watercolors could be included in the exhibition. Of these the Juan Gris *Portrait of Max Jacob* (page 45) is surely the most distinguished. It was recently given to the Museum.

Art historians sometimes seem moved as much by intellectual vanity as by love of truth, critics and museum people by partisanship or love of power, collectors by concern for prestige or the values of the art market or simple pride of possession. I do not find these common foibles in James Soby, who as a scholar, critic, museum worker, and collector seems to me inspired primarily by a love of art and a desire to involve others in the same admirable passion. This love and this desire he has brought, and brings, to the service of the Museum of Modern Art in many ways, on many levels and always with skill, devotion, and generosity of spirit. On shoulders such as his the greatness of an institution rests.

ALFRED H. BARR, JR., *Director of the Museum Collections*

CATALOGUE *with notes by James Thrall Soby*

Some of the notes have been selected or adapted from Mr. Soby's previous publications. These are numbered and listed on page 14 and are referred to in the following pages by the numbers in parentheses and titles.

The artists are arranged in approximately alphabetical order.

The date following each title is that inscribed on the work of art by the artist; when this is not the case, the date is enclosed in parentheses.

Dimensions are in inches; height precedes width. Drawings and watercolors are on paper, and sheet sizes are given, unless otherwise specified.

EUGENE BERMAN. American, born Russia 1899.
The Cart. 1930. Oil on composition board, 45½ x 35½″.
Purchased 1930. (See also page 28)

BACON. *Study for Portrait, Number IV*. (1956)
Oil on canvas, 24¼ x 20". Purchased 1956.

opposite: FRANCIS BACON. British, born 1910. *Study of a Baboon*. 1953. Oil on canvas, 78 x 54". Purchased 1953.

Bacon is fascinated by the drama of contemporary existence as recorded in the pictorial sections of the press. Photographic quotations, thoroughly transformed, are often used in his work. One of his favorite books—"his bible," as a friend of his put it, is Marius Maxwell's *Stalking Big Game with a Camera in Equatorial Africa*, published in 1925 by William Heinemann, Ltd. The photographs are chiefly of large wild animals such as the elephant and the rhinoceros, but among the plates is a remarkable photograph of baboons in acacia trees. The ape at the right is perched on a forked tree trunk extremely like that in Bacon's *Study of a Baboon*. But how to explain the wire cage in which Bacon's ape is half imprisoned? Bacon has traveled often in Africa and the story, probably apocryphal, is that he was fascinated to see monkeys of various kinds caged in the parks, while outside others roamed in freedom.

In 1955–56 Bacon completed a series of "portraits" after J. S. Deville's extraordinary life mask of William Blake in the National Portrait Gallery, London; this is the fourth and final picture in the series.

At intervals throughout his mature career Bacon has made such series of paintings based on images created in the past, the two most extensive being derived from Velasquez' *Pope Innocent X* and van Gogh's portrait of himself on the road to Tarascon. In the Blake series, Bacon, through use of heavy impasto and the scumbled technique of which he is an intensely personal master, has reflected with subtlety the wide, straight mouth and furrowed brow of the great poet, the bulldog-like solidity and determination of his face. For Bacon as for many of his colleagues in British painting today, Blake is a particular hero, both as poet and as artist.

23

BALTHUS (Balthusz Klossowski de Rola). French, born 1908. *The Street*. 1933. Oil on canvas, 6′ 4″ x 7′ 10¼″. Purchased 1937.

"Balthus' first one-man show was held in Paris at the Gallery Pierre in 1934. In that exhibition he included his first large-scale composition, *The Street,* an imaginative transcription of a scene on the rue Bourbon-le-Château in Paris' sixth *arrondissement.* Balthus' first impression of this short street had been recorded in a smaller oil of the same subject, completed in 1929. But whereas the first version retains vestiges of the painter's interest in Bonnard's technique, the large picture abandons impressionism for a stylized, monumental and much more solid handling of color and form. The figures have an hypnotic intensity, as though seen in a dream or viewed on a moving-picture film which abruptly and inexplicably has stopped on its sprockets. It seems likely that at this time Balthus was especially impressed by Seurat's ability to freeze contemporary life at a moment of poetic and age-less dignity; the figure of the chef in *The Street* is closely related to Seurat. The other figures are puppet-like in their sleepwalking irrationality, yet at the same time alive and majestically composed."—(21) *Balthus*

PETER BLUME. American, born Russia 1906.
Key West Beach. 1940. Oil on canvas, 12 x 18". Purchased 1941.

"Blume spent the winter of 1940 at Key West, Florida. There, on the tropical beaches, he found a strange, cacophonous array of rusted stones and gleaming coral, seaweed like wild hair, buoys and rotting chains, all the inexplicable jetsam of the sea. He returned home to paint a series of small oils and to execute numerous pencil drawings of the material he had found. *Key West Beach* is an aggressive manifestation of an imaginative fantasy that Blume had held under more conscious control in earlier works. The color is bright and forceful, the textural manipulation more pronounced than ever before. But what gives it its ultimate distinction is its psychological impact, its obsessive vigor as an image derived from human configuration, however allusive. . . ."—adapted from (12) *Contemporary Painters*

CHRISTIAN BÉRARD. French, 1902–1949.
On the Beach. 1933. Oil on canvas, 31⅞ x 46″. Purchased 1934. Given to The Museum of Modern Art 1960.

In 1933 at Arcachon on the west coast of France near Bordeaux, Bérard painted the double self portrait known as *On the Beach*. It was the largest, most ambitious and quite probably the most sinister of a short series of related pictures completed by the artist in that year.

Bérard had recently seen in Paris a large retrospective Degas show which included paintings of figures on the white sand, their darker belongings strewn around them. He had always revered Degas, and the fine modeling of the heads in his own double portrait suggests comparison with Degas' early portraiture.

On the Beach at first glance appears to consist of two separate images in that the figures and the landscape are oddly disunited, as in certain pictures by Courbet, another Bérard favorite. Yet Bérard's painting flouts cohesion in order to establish a romantic self-absorption that was personal with him. He left few finished pictures. But the finest of these may well earn him a place as the most gifted artist in the Parisian Neo-Romantic group which held its first—and only—exhibition in 1926.

EUGENE BERMAN. American, born Russia 1899.
Memory of Ischia. 1931. Oil on canvas,
38¾ x 31¼". Purchased 1931.

"Berman arrived in Paris in the early 1920's from his native Russia, where, before the Soviet victory, his family had lived in great opulence. . . . For a time, he attended the *Académie Ranson*, where his brother, Léonid, and Christian Bérard were also pupils, and where occasionally the shy, exquisite master, Pierre Bonnard, came to discuss the students' work. With their friend, Pavel Tchelitchew, the young painters were agreed that painting must return to a lyricism of moment and place, and that it must revive the humanist concern with man and his emotions. By 1926, their belief that art should be sensory, rather than primarily cerebral and architectonic, brought them into full reaction against the abstract movement which had begun with cubism. They were soon given the group name, Neo-Romantics, since they clearly exemplified the naturalist side of a romantic revival to which the Surrealists were supplying a somnambulist complement. The title did not altogether please them. It carried connotations of literary dominance from the previous century, and although their inspiration was romantic in mood, all were determined to create a visual order free from literary influence."—(5) *Eugene Berman*

To this day Italy remains the core of Berman's inspiration as an artist. He has returned there repeatedly since his early years, when the island of Ischia in the Bay of Naples prompted him to paint the memorable picture here reproduced.

PIERRE BONNARD. French, 1867–1947. *Grapes*. (c. 1928) Oil on canvas, 16⅝ x 18¼″. Purchased 1932.

Bonnard's unrelenting devotion to craft is typified by a story related by a close friend. For about twenty years one of Bonnard's paintings had hung in the Luxembourg Museum in Paris. Some minor imperfection in the picture troubled the artist, and one day the friend was asked to distract the museum guard while Bonnard took a tiny palette from his pocket and made what he considered to be the necessary alterations. Almost certainly the Luxembourg would have given him permission to work on his picture openly and at leisure, but modesty and the need for privacy were absolutes of his character.

Stemming from the impressionist tradition and perhaps closest in spirit to Claude Monet in the latter's middle years, Bonnard was one of the finest and most subtle colorists of our century. In a picture like *Grapes* he was, as well, extraordinarily daring in compositional matters. The white and black platter which holds the wonderfully iridescent grapes is as boldly conceived as anything by Matisse, who admired Bonnard greatly. For a very long time Bonnard was revered in this country only by a few men of remarkable perceptivity such as Duncan Phillips. Today he has emerged throughout the civilized world as one of the indisputable masters of our time.

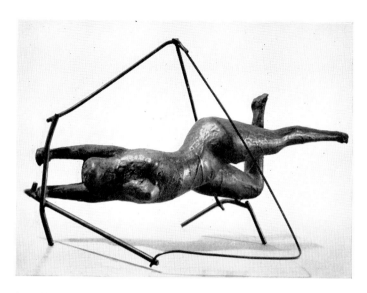

REG BUTLER. British, born 1913. *Figure in Space.* (1956) Bronze, c. 19″ long. Purchased 1956.

Figure in Space. "In this sculpture," said Butler, pointing to the *Figure in Space,* "the figure is the meat, its wire enclosure the gravy. I used to weld and construct my sculptures. Now perhaps because of my rising interest in the human figure, I prefer to have them cast in Paris. It saves my time and energy, and I think it may strengthen my concentration on formal as opposed to mechanical problems."

We were talking in Butler's studio at Berkhamsted Place, about an hour's drive from London. Like others in the amazingly talented group of younger British sculptors who have emerged since the Second World War, Butler proudly admits that it was Henry Moore's international success which helped him believe that England, after so many years of academic ineptitude in sculpture, could produce works of lasting interest in this difficult medium. He is himself the most intellectual member of the newer British group of sculptors (before the war he was a highly-trained metallurgist), and he has grown steadily in certainty and emotional power as an artist.

LYNN CHADWICK. British, born 1914. *Study for the Second Version of "The Seasons."* (1957) Welded iron, plaster and cement, 27½″ high x 13″ wide x 16″ deep. Purchased 1957.

Study for "The Seasons." At the 28th Biennale di Venezia (1956) in the British Pavilion (beautifully installed by Lilian Somerville) Lynn Chadwick was given several galleries and won the first prize for foreign sculpture. Among the pieces he exhibited was a large welded sculpture called *The Seasons* which had been bought by the City Art Museum of St. Louis and which Chadwick had previously sent to an exhibition by that name in London.

Entranced by this particular sculpture, I went to see Chadwick at his farm in Upper Coberley, near Cheltenham, England. He was elated by his Venice award; as his wife explained, "Lynn has never been courted before; he loves it." I told Chadwick how much I liked *The Seasons,* and he replied that he was about to start welding a study for a second version of the St. Louis piece. This is the sculpture here shown. With its pyramidal central form and sprouting branch or foliage it is nearly identical to the original version, though much smaller in scale.

ALEXANDER CALDER. American, born 1898.
Swizzle Sticks. (1936) Mobile of wire, wood and lead against a plywood panel, 48 x 33¼″. Purchased 1937.

It is sometimes difficult to determine the precise sources of inspiration for Calder's mobiles. In the case of *Swizzle Sticks,* a rather unique work of his mid-career, it seems obvious that he had become fascinated by the sticks used to stir champagne. In wood he made enlarged versions of the sticks, weighted them with pieces of lead of different sizes, shapes and weight, balanced them from an armature with that quick and delicate precision he had learned as a student in engineering, and hung them against a plywood panel. As in so many Calder mobiles (and stabiles) the red color used for the panel is called "sign red," and is one of a series known as Ronan's Coach Colors. Calder applies the color with astonishing rapidity and gives it a shimmering liveliness which no one else seems able to duplicate.

Swizzle Sticks is an exceptionally gay work by one of the most gifted and individual American artists of our time.

CALDER. Untitled. (1941) Watercolor, 22 x 30⅝″ (sight). Purchased 1941.

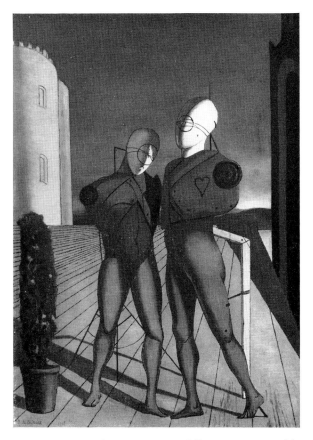

opposite: GIORGIO DE CHIRICO. Italian, born Greece 1888. *Gare Montparnasse (Melancholy of Departure)*. 1914. Oil on canvas, 55⅛ x 72⅝". Purchased 1940.

"The *Gare Montparnasse* is unique in de Chirico's early *oeuvre* in that it portrays an existing, modern structure. Yet in its atmosphere of timelessness the image evokes a sense of a remote, hushed past quite as forcefully as those paintings in which the artist refers, however obliquely, to medieval, Renaissance or neo-classic buildings. And what a strange vision this is! In the foreground a bunch of green bananas inhabits a wasteland of concrete and iron, without plausible exit. This is a station at which presumably no trains will arrive, from which none will depart. The train in the background is approached by the ghosts of two travelers who have climbed the steep ramp only, one imagines, to abandon hope. The silence and inertia are absolute. The picture is the antithesis of paintings by the Italian Futurists in which the commotion and excitement of travel are feverishly suggested.

"According to legend, de Chirico at this time was desperately homesick for Italy and thought often of returning there, only to lose hope because of the costs and complexities of the journey. Certainly the *Gare Montparnasse* is uncannily effective as a dream image of the longings and frustrations of a trip planned by rail (the Montparnasse station was the one nearest to de Chirico's studio on the Left Bank). It conveys the torment of nightmares in which a train must be caught for reasons of exceptional importance. But it also suggests the calm which comes to the traveler when hope of reaching the platform on time has been abandoned, and this ambivalence of mood is characteristic of de Chirico's early art as a whole. . . ."—adapted from (17) *Giorgio de Chirico*

DE CHIRICO. *The Duo*. 1915. Oil on canvas, 32¼ x 23¼". Purchased 1935.

"In *The Duo* the needle-sharp focus of *The Seer* (page 7) is relaxed somewhat and the mood is more poignant. Of all de Chirico's 1915 mannequin series, *The Duo* is the most moving and tender. The lovers in *The Duo* stand out against their elegiac setting like figures seen through a stereoscope. Behind them a green sky frames a rose tower whose soft color and bland texture recall the frescoes of Piero della Francesca. The artificiality of the potted shrub is conveyed with such acuteness that it becomes more real than nature itself. *The Duo* is remarkable for its masterful application of technique to intention, of hand to poetic imagination, of surface communication to those submarine caverns of the mind where the unconscious rolls with the tide, face down."—adapted from (17) *Giorgio de Chirico*

33

DE CHIRICO. *The Enigma of a Day*. 1914. Oil on canvas, 72¾ x 55½". Purchased 1935.

"*The Enigma of a Day* was probably the most important single backdrop used by the Surrealists for the spectacle of their creative activity during the years 1924 to 1935. During those years, the painting hung in the apartment of André Breton, the central figure in the Surrealist movement. He and his colleagues were often photographed in front of the canvas; they propounded a questionnaire asking each other what place in the subconscious the scene represented, how long each had lived there and what its objects meant to them; they made the picture a summary of their aspiration to inhabit the dream. To them it was the embodiment of de Chirico's credo, issued around 1913: 'What I hear is worth nothing; there is only what I see with my eyes open and, even more, what I see with them closed.' In every direction except that of automatism, *The Enigma of a Day* and other works of de Chirico's early career opened the way to Surrealist art in general. They served as well to encourage a revival of human sentiment and atmospheric effect among the Parisian Neo-Romantics of the mid-1920's.

"*The Enigma* is dominated by the Victorian statue in its foreground. De Chirico's interest in the phantomic aspects of public statuary had been aroused in youth by Schopenhauer's words on the subject, and like the philosopher he preferred statues placed low to the ground, so that they seemed to take part in the human procession. After a long search in the major cities of Italy, the writer believes that an actual prototype of *The Enigma*'s sculpture exists; it is the monument to the philosopher, Giovanni Battista Bottero, which stands in Turin's Largo Quattro Marzo. The sculpture is unmistakably late-nineteenth century. Yet it is so painted that its vulgar literalism of costume and pose is made heroic and ageless. The statue takes its place with those of antiquity as the sign of a vanished hour for which the artist's nostalgia is felt."
—adapted from (4) *The Early Chirico* and (17) *Giorgio de Chirico*

35

DE CHIRICO. *The Double Dream of Spring*. 1915. Oil on canvas, 22⅛ x 21⅜". Acquired 1940. Given to The Museum of Modern Art 1957.

"*The Double Dream of Spring* is a companion piece to *The Seer* (page 7) and *The Duo* (page 33), though now only one of the protagonists is a mannequin, the other the Victorian statue so familiar in de Chirico's early art. Both figures seem to have emerged in somnambulism from the shadowed foreground which presumably was the scene of their dreaming. Between them a canvas-within-the-canvas is placed on an easel. Its blue tone is almost identical to the color of the sky, but differentiated from the latter by a subtle greenish overcast. The picture-within-the-picture includes drawings of various components of de Chirico's early iconography—architecture, a

train, a flag, a statue, a landscape, a tower, the legs of the Roman copy of the Hellenistic statue of Ariadne. . . .

"In the background of *The Double Dream of Spring*, the scene of the dream itself is reached by a deep, wooden platform. It is a dream of spring and there is no mistaking it. The sudden warmth in which the diminutive background figures have come out to walk and stand, the restlessness and relief of winter's end—these are conveyed with a persuasiveness that goes far beyond the limits of traditional realism, and once again we are reminded of the painter's avowed intention to record the emotional impact of imagined experience rather than to document external appearances. His example opened the way for Surrealist artists such as Ernst, Tanguy, Magritte, Dali and Delvaux whose debt to de Chirico all have proudly acknowledged."—adapted from (17) *Giorgio de Chirico*

DE CHIRICO. *The Amusements of a Young Girl.* (1916?)
Oil on canvas, 18½ x 15¾″. Purchased 1940.

"One of the most brilliant of de Chirico's Ferrarese works
is *The Amusements of a Young Girl.* There is little precedent in de Chirico's early art for the Courbet-like solidity of the modeling of the leather glove, and not until
1919 in the Museum of Modern Art's famous picture,
The Sacred Fish, did the artist's technique again become
so thoroughly sensuous. Yet there is every reason to believe that the picture was finished at Ferrara, where de
Chirico was confined to a military hospital during the
First World War; its date must be 1916 or 1917, probably the former. The building in the background is obvi-
ously Ferrara's red Castello Estense; the box of matches in
the foreground is labelled 'Ferrara'; the handling of the
architecture, the flooring and the board on which the
glove is pinned indicates a 1916 or 1917 date. Certainly
the picture was completed before the end of the war and
long before de Chirico's growing interest in Courbet
prompted him to write a monograph on the French master (published in 1925). Whatever its exact date, *The
Amusements of a Young Girl* is one of the handsomest
and most condensed of all the painter's many still-life
compositions."—adapted from (17) *Giorgio de Chirico*

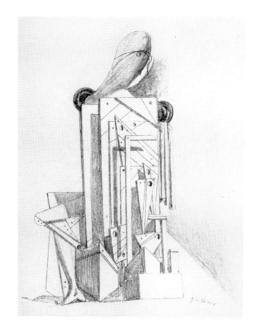

DE CHIRICO. *The Faithful Servitor.* (1916 or 1917) Oil on canvas, 15⅛ x 13⅝". Purchased c. 1935.

DE CHIRICO. *The Condottiere.* (1917) Pencil, 11¼ x 8⅜" (sight). Purchased c. 1935.

The Faithful Servitor. "Did the fact that during the First World War de Chirico was obliged to spend much of his time in the military hospital at Ferrara have an effect on his art? It seems more than likely that this was indeed the case and that his rising nervous instability, as the tragedy of the war assumed greater proportions, is reflected in several still lifes of this time for which the word 'claustrophobic' does not seem too strong. In *The Faithful Servitor,* for example, there is a new emphasis on forms descending from the top of the picture space or crowding in from the sides, as though the artist felt abnormally depressed by his confinement in the hospital for neuropsychiatric reasons.

"It seems possible, too, that the edible objects which appear so often in de Chirico's still lifes of the Ferrarese period may have a symbolic significance; such objects may have represented in his distraught mind the delicacies of civilian life. In *The Faithful Servitor* these objects—biscuits in their glittering wrappings—assume a luxuriousness of tone and texture, as if the painter's longing for the

amenities of normal existence had become especially deep. . . ."—adapted from (17) *Giorgio de Chirico*

Grand Metaphysical Interior (opposite). "One of the climactic and most widely reproduced of de Chirico's Ferrarese still lifes is the *Grand Metaphysical Interior,* one of the richest works in color of his entire early career. To the right are hung what appear to be window shades like those commonly seen in Neapolitan houses and shop fronts. At the left is a framed picture-within-the-picture, with landscape and a road winding past a fountain and a typically Italian resort hotel toward a distant lake or bay, bathed in sunlight. . . . The richly painted landscape is a long cry from the arid impasto of the artist's architectural scenes of 1913–14. De Chirico's new emphasis on realistic modeling is nowhere better exemplified than in the handling of the crusted *brioches* within their boxed frame. The *Grand Metaphysical Interior* proposes an unforgettable counterplay between realism of detail and fantasy of over-all invention."—(17) *Giorgio de Chirico*

38

DE CHIRICO. *Grand Metaphysical Interior.* 1917. Oil on canvas, 37¾ x 27⅜″. Purchased 1935.

CHARLES DEMUTH. American, 1883–1935.
Female Acrobats. 1916. Watercolor,
12½ x 7½″ (sight). Purchased 1945.

JOSEPH CORNELL. American, born 1903. *Taglioni's Jewel Casket*. 1940.
Wooden box containing glass ice cubes, jewelry, etc., 11⅞ x 8¼ x 4¾″.
Purchased 1941. Given to The Museum of Modern Art 1953.

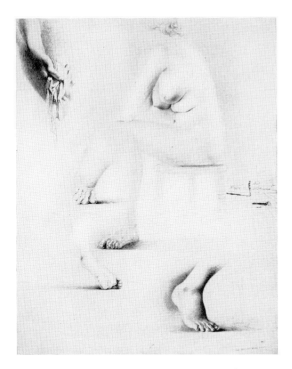

SALVADOR DALI. Spanish, born 1904. *Nude.* 1935. Pencil, 6¾ x 5½". Purchased 1935.

DALI. *Debris of an automobile giving birth to a blind horse biting a telephone.* 1938. Oil on canvas, 21¼ x 25½". Purchased 1939.

"Whenever possible Dali has made living organism usurp, jeopardize or obviate the function of machinery and machine products; whenever possible he has forced the inanimate to take part in action for which the essential requisite is animation itself. The tendency is illustrated by such a painting as the *Debris of an automobile.* . . . The automobile is here given the ability to reproduce not itself but the horse, which in contemporary civilization it has driven off the streets, but which now seems to emerge triumphant from the wreck of industrialism. The horse releases its fury by biting a telephone, a mechanical instrument which Dali considers so disastrous in connotation that at the time of the Munich Conference, arranged by telephone, he made the instrument the iconographical center of several paintings. . . ."

—(3) *Salvador Dali*

JEAN DUBUFFET. French, born 1901. *My Cart, My Garden*. 1955. Oil on canvas, 35 x 45¾". Purchased 1956.

Since his first one-man exhibition in Paris in 1944, Dubuffet has always been anti-art in its traditional sense of exalted beauty and skill. His most celebrated dictum in this regard is as follows: "The merit which we Occidental nations attribute to art and the attention lavished on it tend to substitute a specious product which is the counterfeit of art. Too highly honored, art is rarely nowadays a free celebration. . . . It has become, instead, a game of ceremonies which leads it into alien terrain. . . . Its true and only terrain is rapture and delirium; it is extra-curricular and doesn't belong in the school schedule."

For all his defiance of established canons and despite the often extreme unconventionality of his technical methods, Dubuffet has emerged as perhaps the most compelling, certainly the most idiosyncratic of postwar French painters. If sometimes his art does indeed "dance and yell like a madman," it is nevertheless marked by an inescapable profundity of vision. A picture such as *My Cart, My Garden*, with its close harmonies of brownish color and scratched texture, seems to fulfill Dubuffet's faith—"that a painting could be both a vast landscape and at the same time a tiny patch of dust seen through a microscope." The picture is one of the artist's own particular favorites, a fact which, as with most artists, may or may not be of significance.

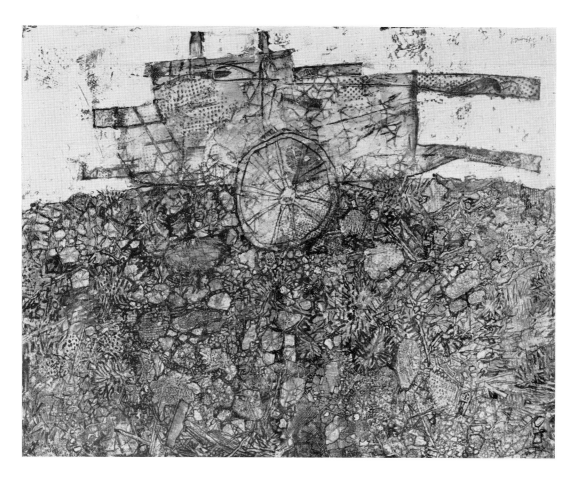

MAX ERNST. French, born Germany 1891. *Alice in 1941.* 1941. Oil on canvas, 15¾ x 12½″. Purchased 1942.

During the early stages of the Second World War, Ernst, as a German, was confined for a time to a French concentration camp. The surrounding terrain was apparently mountainous, the military discipline not too severe for men like Ernst, whose devotion to France—their adopted homeland—was a matter of long and consistent record. In the camp Ernst began to paint *Alice in 1941,* its single human figure being an "imagined" portrait of a painter-friend, Leonora Carrington, then a colleague in the Surrealist movement.

Presently Ernst was released by the French authorities and came to America where he was married to the celebrated patroness of the arts, Miss Peggy Guggenheim. For a time he and his wife lived in Arizona, whose arid, craggy landscape delighted the painter and where he completed *Alice in 1941,* making immensely skilled use of the decalcomania technique which had long interested him as one of the most versatile and inventive technicians in contemporary art.

ALBERTO GIACOMETTI. Swiss, born 1901. *Tall Figure.* (1949) Painted bronze, 65⅝″ high. Purchased 1957.

right: JUAN GRIS. Spanish, 1887–1927.
Portrait of Max Jacob. 1919. Pencil, 14⅜ x 10½″. Purchased 1932. Given to The Museum of Modern Art 1958.

below: GRIS. *Still Life.* 1916.
Pencil, 15⅛ x 10¾″ (sight). Purchased 1932.

Giacometti: Tall Figure (opposite). "In the mid-1930's Giacometti began to work from the model, day after day for five years, hardly ever satisfied and destroying much of what he produced. Then he tried working from memory. 'But wanting to create from memory what I had seen, to my terror the sculptures became smaller and smaller, they only had a likeness when very small, yet their dimensions revolted me, and tirelessly I began again and again. . . . A large figure seemed to me untrue and a small one intolerable. . . . All this changed a little in 1945 through drawing. This led me to want to make larger figures, and then to my surprise they achieved a resemblance only when long and slender.' "—(24) *Modern Art and the New Past*

The *Tall Figure* is long and slender indeed! In fact it seems to confirm Jean Paul Sartre's opinion of Giacometti: "to sculpt for him, is to take the fat off space." It is also one of those fantastically attenuated standing figures which magnetize the surrounding air and light, attracting to themselves an inexplicably poetic nimbus. This is the third in a series of six bronze casts of the same figure and in patina the most enriched by paint.

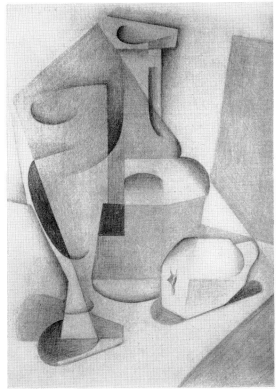

opposite: GRACE HARTIGAN. American, born 1922. *Shinnecock Canal.* 1957. Oil on canvas, 7′ 6½″ x 6′ 4″. Purchased 1957. Given to The Museum of Modern Art 1960.

"I asked Miss Hartigan first which artists of the past and present had meant most to her. She replied that she didn't feel particularly related to any painter, though she had learned from many. She added: 'In a sense I had to make my own art history, to paint it out for three or four years. I felt I didn't have the right to freedom, but had to win it for myself. Lots of artists can assume a heritage, especially the Europeans, but I wanted to discover mine and to believe in something beyond the act of painting. I also wanted to find out whether it was necessary for a contemporary American painter to come out of the French tradition, and therefore for several years I concentrated on the Spanish masters in the Metropolitan Museum and the Hispanic Museum in New York.'

"I asked then why she had produced a number of *collages.* 'Because,' she said, 'the pasted-on forms let me pick images out of the world, very real and pure, with no memory associations. My *Montauk Highway* and *Shinnecock Canal* stem from these *collages,* which are mainly of subjects that interested me when driving—in the Four Roses whiskey billboards, for example, a rose is as big as a human head. Our highways are fantastic; I like nature as imposed on by man. Most of all I like to work directly from American sources and phenomena.' "—"Interview with Grace Hartigan," *Saturday Review,* October 5, 1957

JASPER JOHNS. American, born 1930. *White Target.* 1957. Encaustic on canvas, 30 x 30″. Purchased 1958.

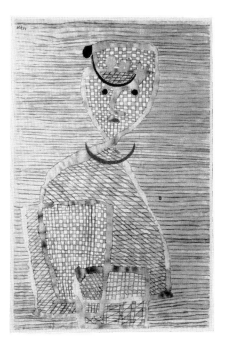

PAUL KLEE. German, 1879–1940; born and died in Switzerland. *Gifts for I.* 1928. Tempera on gesso on canvas mounted on wood, 15¾ x 22″. Purchased 1932.

KLEE. *Schoolgirl.* (1930) Watercolor, 19¼ x 12⅜″. Purchased 1944.

"Klee was the vigilant ally of accidental beauty, ready to intervene with quick and unfailing instinct on the side of poetic chance.

"His art, even at its most fantastic, was infrequently to sever completely its nervous and acute contact with reality. His images, even when most hallucinatory or abstract, seldom lost their suggestion of sharply personal remembrance and actual experience transformed. Something happened to Klee before he executed each of his paintings, something was said or seen or imagined anew —and this in an age when many artists have formalized repeatedly the same experience or vision. In nearly every instance, his art was quick with a new and particular life. . . . His wit was spontaneous, varied to extraordinary degree and wonderfully controlled. Indeed, it would be difficult to think of another artist of recent times whose humor is so thoroughly fused with a visual medium. His titles contribute enormously, of course, and were in most cases inscribed on the pictures by the artist so that they might not be lost. But even without titles, innumerable of his works are magnificently and instantly witty. He is that rarest of comedians who provokes laughter before he has opened his mouth. Faced by his works, one may easily agree to his quotation from Gogol: 'There is a laughter which is to be put on the same dignified level as higher lyrical emotion, and which is as distant as heaven from the convulsions of a vulgar clown.'"—(8) *The Prints of Paul Klee*

According to Alfred Flechtheim, for many years Klee's German dealer, *Gifts for I.*, with its champagne glass, table, salt shaker and toppled head, commemorates a festive party given for or by one of Klee's close friends.

48

LÉONID (Léonid Berman). American, born Russia 1896. *Mussel Gatherers at High Tide*. 1937. Oil on canvas, 21¼ x 32″. Purchased 1937.

"Léonid's preference in seascape is for those places in which water, land and sky are in close and ancient communion; he has no interest whatever in the ocean for its own sake or in those dramatic episodes of tempest admired by marine painters of an earlier time. His taste is confirmed by minute and sometimes oblique details. When, for example, he stands beside his *Mussel Gatherers at High Tide*, he will first describe the exceptional flavor of the mussels scraped from the wooden weirs in his picture. . . . His appreciation of a given fishing village extends to its people, boats and gear, to the sweep of its beach or the angle of its jetties. Once in Paris he drew with relish a map of the French harbors where he had worked, remembering the paintings he had derived from each."—"Léonid," *Horizon*, Vol. XX, no. 119, London, 1949

LÉONID. *The Fisherwoman*. (1930) Oil on wood, 11¼ x 9¼″. Purchased 1932.

49

WILHELM LEHMBRUCK. German, 1881–1919.
Torso. (1913–14). Cast stone, 36½″ high. Acquired
1933.

Lehmbruck's *Torso* (*opposite*) was part of the collection
of the artist's works taken from his Paris studio in 1914,
sequestered by the French Government as enemy prop-
erty, Lehmbruck being a German, and later sold at the
Hôtel Drouot (1921).

In 1933 August Hoff, then Director of the Lehmbruck
Museum in Duisburg, Germany, wrote the Marie Harri-
man Gallery in New York, at that time the owners of the
Torso, to say that his museum owned a bronze cast of the
piece and that a second version of the cast stone sculpture, "where the bones are longer," existed. Otherwise
he knew of no other cast in any material. The *Torso* here
shown was for a time in the celebrated collection of Dr.
Reber of Lausanne, Switzerland. It is remarkable for that
pensive grace and nervous subtlety of modeling which
have made Lehmbruck, despite his tragically short career,
one of the most respected sculptors of our time.

LEHMBRUCK. *Woman's Head.* (c. 1910) Cast stone,
16½″ high. Purchased 1932.

right: ARISTIDE MAILLOL. French,
1861–1944. *Leda.* (c. 1902) Bronze,
11¼″ high. Purchased c. 1930.

far right: MAILLOL. *Woman Arranging
Her Hair.* (c. 1898) Bronze, 10¾″ high.
Purchased c. 1930.

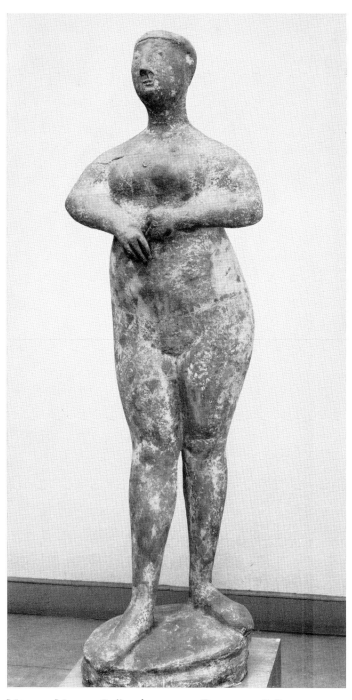

"Marini's studio is in the courtyard below his apartment in Milan. There he models in plaster, or very rarely carves, his majestic and unforgettable figures, arriving repeatedly at an eloquent balance between raw power and lyric delicacy. 'It is necessary,' he says, 'to preserve the emotion which generates an image. You cannot do so by posing a model, for then you get lost in details that weaken or discolor the original emotion. My sculpture starts from an impression, often instantaneous, whose impact I try to preserve. I include details only if they confirm the impact, as in the case of the rings on the fingers of this woman in bronze—very Italian. I saw the woman herself in the fields, a large woman with powerful legs. She stood like this, and I remembered her, and now here is her sculpture.'

"Thus while many of Marini's elders have been concerned with pure form on the one hand, with the re-creation of myth on the other, he customarily takes his impetus from living incident. . . . He once said: 'One must explore and know, before one can sing.' His own voice is one of the deepest and clearest in the newer European art scene."—*Marino Marini*, foreword to exhibition catalogue, Buchholz Gallery, 1950

MARINI. *Standing Nudes*. (1948) Ink and wash, 11¼ x 8¼" (sight). Gift of the artist 1948.

MARINO MARINI. Italian, born 1901. *Dancer*. 1948. Bronze (cast 1949), 69½" high. Purchased 1949.

MARINI. *The Horseman.* (1946–47)
Bronze, 34½″ high. Purchased 1948.

" 'To be an artist is simple,' Marini once said. 'It is simplicity which is difficult. In Italy so much is truly simple —the land, the people. Our discipline is not like that of the North; it is far less intellectual. Yet I suppose I am myself Nordic, a little. At any rate, I believe in cultivation as a protection against confusion. It is impossible to pretend to be a primitive. You asked me, for instance, about the sculpture of China. It is one of the great sources, like the art of Egypt, and of course I admire it.'

"We were talking in Marini's modern apartment in Milan, a city which favors his intense working schedule because it provides a surrounding contemporary energy, of life and industry. . . . If native tradition has long since ceased to be a pressing need for his own development, he knows much about the Italian past. Gradually he mentioned some of his enthusiasms: the equestrian monument to Marcus Aurelius in the Piazza del Campidoglio at Rome; the medieval sculpture of Giovanni Pisano and Tino da Camaino; the huge wooden horse that served as the model for Donatello's *Gattamelata;* the paintings of Paolo Uccello. In nearly everything Marini admires is to be found a swift, frank vigor—so dominant a quality in his own personality as an artist.

"As long ago as 1936 Marini started his series of horsemen, but his full realization of the theme began after he had seen the Lombard peasants fleeing the British bombings on their frightened horses."—*Marino Marini,* foreword to exhibition catalogue, Buchholz Gallery, 1950

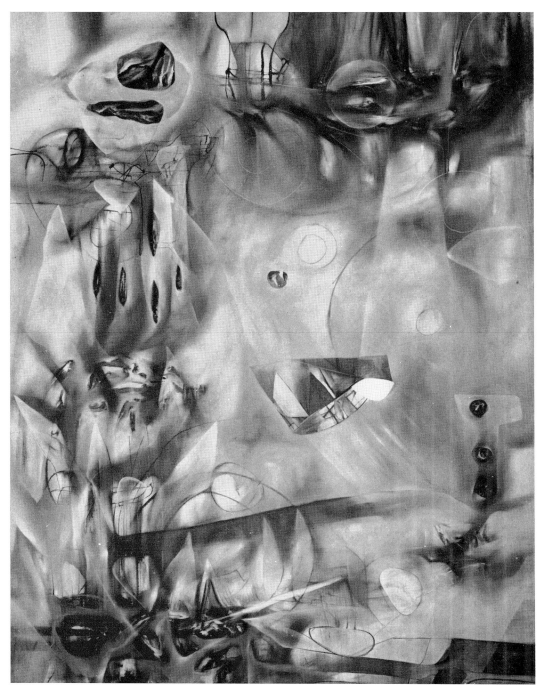

MATTA (Sebastian Antonio Matta Echaurren). Chilean, born 1912. *Here Sir Fire, Eat!* (1942) Oil on canvas, 56 x 44″. Acquired 1944.

MATTA. *Joan of Arc.* (1942) Colored pencil and crayon, 23½ x 29¼″ (irregular). Purchased 1942.

above: MATTA. *The Disasters of Mysticism.* 1942. Oil on canvas, 38¼ x 51⅜″. Purchased 1943.

The Disasters of Mysticism. "In youth Matta studied to be an architect in Le Corbusier's Paris office, and at that time visited England. Did he admire there the late paintings of Turner? He speaks casually of Turner's art, with no marked respect, yet among paintings of modern times Turner's are perhaps nearest in spirit to Matta's early works, with two important exceptions—Kandinsky's free improvisations of 1911–18 and Miró's untypical but impressive *Still Life with Old Shoe.* As to Matta's connection with earlier sources, his veiled hills, jets of fire and rolling fogs are related, however distantly, to the sixteenth-century nocturnal mysticism exemplified by such separate works as Grünewald's *Temptation of St. Anthony* panel at Colmar and Beccafumi's *Victory of St. Michael* at Siena. Significantly, his tissues of flaming color have often assumed the Mannerist forms of El Greco, as in *The Disasters of Mysticism.*"—adapted from (12) *Contemporary Painters*

MIRÓ. *Still Life with Old Shoe*. 1937. Oil on canvas, 32 x 46″. Acquired 1944. (Reproduced page 17)

"In 1937 Miró, perhaps as a deliberate foil to Picasso's magnificent *Guernica*, produced a work unique in his career as an easel painter: the *Still Life with Old Shoe*, a tragic and forceful summary of his emotions about the [Spanish Civil] war.

"Pierre Loeb, at that time Miró's Paris dealer, has said that the artist set up on a table . . . an actual still life consisting of an apple pierced by tines, a gin bottle with paper wrapping, a loaf of bread, and an old shoe, and painted it all of every day for a month. (Afterwards Miró took the picture back to his new studio on the rue Blanqui to finish; it is dated on the back January 24–May 29, 1937.) For the melancholy protest Miró wished to make against Spain's poverty and suffering, a return to the realism of his early career must have seemed necessary. The colors are dark and lurid. In the sky a ghostly silhouette floats in from the left, the bottle itself casts a heavy shadow and ominous black clouds fill the upper right section. The apple is savagely impaled by the fork, the loaf of bread's carved end becomes a skull, and even

the gin bottle with its grimacing letters, G I, seems menaced by the upheld, ragged ends of its own wrapping. The more gentle colors of the old shoe do nothing to obviate its vitality as a symbol of need; the callouses and wrinkles of long wear are effectively defined, and one senses the weariness of the foot it once encased.

"To create so memorable a polemic work of art in terms of still life is a very considerable achievement, not unworthy of its allegorical companion piece, Picasso's *Guernica*."—adapted from (27) *Joan Miró*

Portrait of Mrs. Mills in 1750. "In 1929 Miró's most ambitious if short series of paintings consisted of 'imaginary' portraits of female figures from the past, including . . . *Portrait of Mrs. Mills in 1750*. We now know from the artist himself that this picture was paraphrased from John R. Smith's engraving of a *Portrait of Mrs. Mills* by George Engleheart, a pupil of Sir Joshua Reynolds. The interrelationship between Miró's image and Engleheart's is striking. In both paintings the figure wears a large hat; in both she holds out a white sheaf of paper which in the Engleheart is a letter and in the Miró either that or a sheet of music. (In actual life Mrs. Mills was a singer.) . . .

"Precisely why Miró should have been beguiled by such figures from the art of the past is not a matter of clear record, despite questioning of the artist himself by several friends and critics, among them the writer. It seems possible that he had become interested in the curvilinear forms of earlier epochs . . . which reached a late climax in the *art nouveau* style. Moreover, the biomorphic character of the contours in Miró's 1929 'portraits' suggests some influence from his good friend—and in 1925–26 his close neighbor—Jean (Hans) Arp, who had already invented a whole new vocabulary of living as opposed to geometric shapes . . . though Arp has denied vehemently that he ever influenced his younger friend, insisting that Miró arrived at his style by quite another route—the art of children and the early Catalan frescoes. In any case, the most impressive picture in the 1929 series is the *Portrait of Mrs. Mills in 1750*, with its rich chocolate browns, reds, greens, purples, and blacks, its beautifully soft texture which was indeed . . . inspired by Catalan wall paintings."—adapted from (27) *Joan Miró*

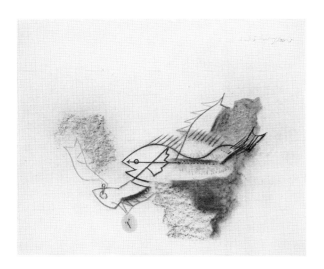

ANDRÉ MASSON. French, born 1896. *Study for "Battle of Fishes."* (1927) Pastel, 18¼ x 22⅞″ (sight). Purchased 1932.

JOAN MIRÓ. Spanish, born 1893. *Portrait of Mrs. Mills in 1750*. 1929. Oil on canvas, 45½ x 35″. Purchased 1943.

MIRÓ. *Collage*. 1934. Collage on sandpaper, 14½ x 9¼". Purchased 1935.

"In 1937–38, Miró executed a masterful self portrait (*opposite*), in which color is reduced to minor accents and the drawing is hypnotically intense and skilled. The image is at once a triumph of self-examination and a technical *tour de force* of the finest order. It is also a virtual anthology of those cryptic forms—stars, pinwheels, and inexplicable objects—of which the artist has always been fond. . . . The staring pinwheel eyes dominate the head; the fluted stylizations of the nose, upper lip, and chin are original and sensitive. Throughout the image are embedded baubles in the shape of sunbursts and starfish, like useless but treasured objects on a nursery shelf. . . .

"Certain critics have wondered why Miró, so superb a colorist, used so little color in the *Self Portrait*. (Significantly, it was at this time that the artist first became engrossed in making etchings and aquatints, and their calligraphy almost certainly had some effect on his linear preoccupations in the *Self Portrait*.) . . . According to an eye witness, Pierre Matisse, the picture was done in a small room in Miró's apartment on the rue Blanqui. On one side of the room Miró had hung a round, convex mirror whose magnification undoubtedly affected the artist's drawing and accounts at least in part for the image's looming monumentality, its glacial aggrandizements. On the other side of the room Miró placed his easel, and during the entire time the picture was being painted turned back and forth from mirror to canvas. When the portrait was completed he decided to try his hand at a second and much more colorful version. He therefore traced the composition on another canvas of the same size and pondered the problem of strengthening the tonal brilliance. He quickly came to the conclusion that the original version was complete in itself, and the tracing was abandoned. . . ."—(27) *Joan Miró*

58

MIRÓ. *Self Portrait.* 1937–38.
Pencil, crayon and oil on canvas,
57½ x 38¼″. Purchased 1949.

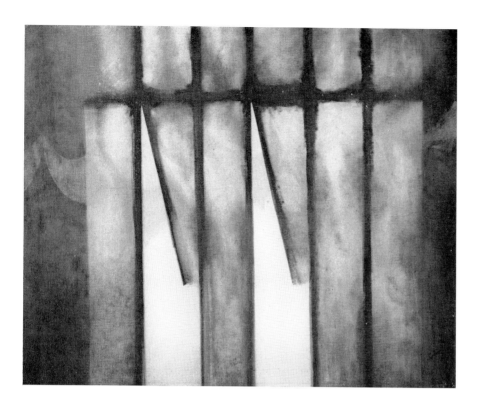

left: LOREN MacIVER. American, born 1909.
Skylight. (1948) Oil on canvas, 40¼ x 48¼".
Purchased 1948.

below: MacIVER. Tree. (1945)
Oil on canvas, 40 x 25⅞". Purchased 1946.

"MacIver seems to find her subjects everywhere: everywhere, that is, except where traditional visual excitements might be expected to come into play. Grandeur in all its aspects leaves her cold, as does pre-established elegance and other forms of drama. She has developed her own thoroughly private sense of the picturesque; she has emphasized the unassertive phenomena of daily existence; she particularly likes disused objects and abandoned vestiges of ritualistic moment. . . . The truth about MacIver (and it is a lovely truth) is that her attention wanders. No one can predict from one moment to the next what will catch her attention as a painter; we can only be certain that it will be something everyone else has overlooked."—(24) *Modern Art and the New Past*

Tree was inspired by the sight of a privet hedge beginning to blossom in front of a church on Perry Street, New York, where MacIver lives. "We so miss trees in New York," she says, "and the hedge seemed to take their place."

60

GIORGIO MORANDI. Italian, born 1890. *Still Life*. 1949.
Oil on canvas, 13½ x 17″. Purchased 1949.

Morandi: Still Life. "To realize fully the dedication of
Morandi's career, it is perhaps most of all helpful to see
the room in which he works at Bologna. The bottles and
other containers which engross him are stacked everywhere in fantastic number, and some of them Morandi
has ornamented with squares and rectangles which he
may or may not transpose in painting his canvases. His
taste in these objects runs from expensive vials to gas-
station cartons for oil, from Oriental tins of tea to hum-
ble, local jugs. No one can predict or explain how and
why his final choice of still-life elements is made, but
certainly it involves an intense and poetic imaginative
process. What this process is, and how it functions, no
one is likely to find out from Morandi himself. A large,
taciturn man, his modesty is so extreme that often he
signs his canvases at their very edge, as though it troubled
him to take credit for what he has created.

"It takes a long time to appreciate the purity of
Morandi's achievement—about as long as it takes to com-
prehend the transcendental compulsions of Piet Mon-
drian, his non-representational counterpart in steady devotion to solving the most delicate problems of order and
form."—"Giorgio Morandi," *Saturday Review*, January
4, 1958

HENRY MOORE. British, born 1898.
Ideas for Sculpture. 1942.
Watercolor, 14⅞ x 9¾″. Purchased 1943.

MARCELLO MUCCINI. Italian, born 1926.
Vespignani and Graziella Urbinati. 1948.
Charcoal, 24½ x 15¾″. Purchased 1948.

PICASSO. *Nude Seated on a Rock.* (1921)
Tempera on wood, 5⅞ x 3⅞".
Purchased 1935.

One of the many fascinations in studying Picasso's neo-classic paintings of 1920 to 1924 is to try to understand why the artist should have been interested in such drastic extremes of format. In 1920 he painted the large *Two Seated Women* in the Chrysler collection; the following year he finished the *Nude Seated on a Rock* which is roughly the size of a postcard and yet is quite closely related to a very big painting in which the pose of the figure is nearly identical and which was finished at about the same time. It is typical of Picasso's extraordinary facility and certitude in questions of scale that the figures in both paintings should appear equally monumental and that their discrepant formats should seem inevitable.

The little *Nude Seated on a Rock* had been presented by the artist to a member of his family, but was most generously released to me when A. Everett Austin, Jr. and I organized the large retrospective Picasso exhibition at the Wadsworth Atheneum in Hartford, Connecticut, in 1934.

PABLO PICASSO. French, born Spain 1881. *Seated Woman.* 1927. Oil on wood, 51⅛ x 38¼". Purchased 1932. (Frontispiece)

In his *Picasso: Fifty Years of his Art,* Alfred Barr wrote: "Picasso's power of inventing masks is here remarkably demonstrated: a great curving band sweeps upward to terminate in the frightening white profile which is then both intersected and magically extended by the black axe-bladed, disk-eyed shadow. This is one of the most awe-inspiring of all Picasso's figure paintings." It is indeed so awe-inspiring that since I bought it in 1932, I have been asked repeatedly how I could possibly live with such a ferocious and demanding image. The only answer I can make is that one does not look constantly at a picture this powerful, any more than one plays Stravinsky on the victrola from morning until night. For weeks on end I look away from the *Seated Woman.* And then turn back to it with the awe it was meant to inspire.

After his series of serenely handsome still lifes of the mid–1920's, Picasso began to heighten the psychological impact of his work in the famous *Three Dancers* of 1925, as has often been pointed out. He had almost certainly been affected by the aims of the Surrealists who now became his friends. He never officially joined their movement, yet in a very real sense he dominated its art through his relentless energy and unflagging invention.

PICASSO. *The Sigh*. 1923. Oil and charcoal on canvas, 23¾ x 19¾″. Purchased 1931.

During the early 1920's Picasso was living in considerable splendor and elegance on the rue la Boétie in Paris. Perhaps the new luxuriousness of his life, plus his interest in ballet, accounts in part for the gentle sweetness and almost romantic mood of *The Sigh*, its deliberate and courageous dandyism in an era when most artists were afraid of sentiment and fashion.

The Sigh is among other things a remarkable *tour de force*. The figure, the chair and the cane seem to have been drawn with headlong certainty, without visible corrections of any kind; the patches of thin color are restrained and deft. The picture probably horrified the more harsh and dogmatic of the artist's former Bohemian colleagues. But then, as he once remarked, "Do these people think I paint only for them?"

SHAHN. *Girl Jumping Rope.* (1943) Ink, 22 x 30″. Gift of the artist 1945.

left: BEN SHAHN. American, born Russia 1898. *Father and Child.* 1946. Tempera on cardboard mounted on wood, 40 x 29⅞″. Purchased 1946. Given to The Museum of Modern Art 1957.

As often happens in Shahn's art some of the objects shown in *Father and Child* are family possessions. The woman's embroidered skirt belonged to the artist's wife, Bernarda; the photograph she carries away from the ruined village is a portrait of an ancestor; the man's white gloves are the cotton workmen's gloves of which Shahn is fond. The burnt-out village was probably inspired by photographs the painter had seen of Europe's wartime ruins.

SHAHN. *Liberation.* 1945. Tempera on composition board, 29¾ x 39¾″. Purchased 1945. (Reproduced on cover)

"Did Shahn's sympathy for the people of Europe during the Second World War lead him nearer to European sources of art? At any rate, his paintings of the war years are often linked as never before to those foreign artists, from the fourteenth-century Sienese through Fra Angelico to the seventeenth-century brothers Le Nain, whose vision was distinguished by a kind of elegant humility. At that time he progressed to a closer communion with lyric world tradition, though sacrificing none of his originality or vigor. The pole in *Liberation* is as bright and enchanted as a maypole by Ambrogio Lorenzetti; the child at the left of the composition is like an early Renaissance angel of Annunciation.

"Shahn's paintings of the 1940's still derive their vitality from the humanism and love of truth which engendered his first mature works. He painted *Liberation* only after he had seen children swinging wildly in his yard, half in pleasure and half in pop-eyed fear of falling, when it was announced that France was free again. The children's legs are piercingly real in weight and flourish. The picture's architectural rubble was probably inspired by photographs of Europe's ruined buildings, but was painted from a handful of gravel brought in from Shahn's driveway."—adapted from (10) *Ben Shahn*

GRAHAM SUTHERLAND. British, born 1903. *Thorn Head*. 1945. Chalk, ink and gouache, 22 x 21". Purchased 1946.

Sutherland: Thorn Head. "During the earlier 1940's Graham Sutherland's preoccupation with thorn trees and bushes sprang from his interest in painting a Crucifixion, completed in 1946, for the Church of St. Matthew in Northampton, England. Quite typically, he reduced his initial conception to minutiae which typified for him the point of sharpest psychological focus in the tremendous scene to be represented. He went to the core of drama, so to speak, and the many paintings he made of thorns prepared the portent of the Crucifixion itself. He did not, however, entirely surrender abstract form to expressionist emotion. In describing his ideological concern with thorns, he mentioned, too, his search for a biomorphic order—'A sort of pricking and demarkation of a hollow headshaped space enclosed by the points.' It was the head of Christ that eventually filled this space, but only after long, relatively formal experiment with contour and volume."—(12) *Contemporary Painters*

Sage: Watching the Clock. "Kay Sage lived in Italy for many years; she speaks of it often and dearly. And among modern artists she greatly admires the Italian de Chirico ('metaphysical' period) and her late husband, Yves Tanguy. De Chirico and Tanguy! These are formidable personalities to hold in respect. A lesser painter would have surrendered her identity to their spell. Kay Sage, on the contrary, has watched and listened and profited—and gone her separate way. Her art creates its own silence: lovely, serene and memorable. She has painted since childhood, but her technical progress in recent years has been astonishing. But who thinks of her paintings in terms of technique? Not I. Nor you, if you would understand them best."—*Kay Sage*, preface to retrospective exhibition catalogue, Galleria dell' Obelisco, Rome, 1953

Watching the Clock was shot at her request by a gunsmith, who is her neighbor and friend in Woodbury, Connecticut, probably as a Surrealist defiance of the sanctity of the hand-painted easel picture.

KAY SAGE. American, born 1898. *Watching the Clock*. 1958. Oil on canvas, 14 x 14". Gift of the artist 1958.

65

The Furniture of Time (opposite). "After a voyage to Africa (1929?), Tanguy usually substituted mineral forms for the vegetal ones used in earlier works. His color became more complex and varied, with extremes of light and dark replacing the relatively even tonality of his previous pictures. At the same time he made more and more frequent use of one of his most poetic inventions—the melting of land into sky, one image metamorphosed into another, as in the moving-picture technique known as lap-dissolve. The fixed horizon was now often replaced by a continuous and flowing treatment of space, and in many paintings of the 1930's and 1940's, among them *The Furniture of Time*, it is extremely difficult to determine at what point earth becomes sky or whether objects rest on the ground or float aloft. The ambiguity is intensified by changes in the density of the objects themselves, from opaque to translucent to transparent, creating a spatial *double entendre*."—(18) Yves Tanguy

"Though recognizing that Surrealism as a cohesive movement was ended, in his last years Tanguy remained faithful to its insistence on vaulting obsolete barriers to human consciousness. But he always held back from the polemical activities of his colleagues, and however firmly he was committed to Surrealism's purposeful anti-esthetic, he remained in some measure a classical French artist, with or without his own consent in the matter. Indeed, when he held his volume of Montaigne and said of it 'everything is here,' one sensed what I trust the future will confirm—that Tanguy is the spiritual heir of Chardin no less than of Surrealism's literary hero, Isidore Ducasse, Comte de Lautréamont."—"Inland in the Subconscious: Yves Tanguy," *Magazine of Art*, Vol. 42, no. 1, January 1949

above: YVES TANGUY. American, born France. 1900–1955. *The Mood of Now* (*L'Humeur des temps*). 1928. Oil on canvas, 39⅜ x 28⅞″. Purchased 1955.

left: TANGUY. Untitled. 1947. Gouache, 13⅛ x 9½″. Purchased 1948.

TANGUY. *The Furniture of Time* (*Le Temps meublé*). 1939. Oil on canvas, 45¾ x 35″. Purchased 1943.

PAVEL TCHELITCHEW. American, born Russia. 1898–1957. *Blue Clown*. 1929. Oil on canvas, 31¾ x 23⅝″. Purchased 1934.

TCHELITCHEW. *Cabbage Head*. 1939. Gouache and ink, 16⅝ x 12¾″. Purchased 1939.

Blue Clown. "Tchelitchew's metamorphic paintings of 1928–29 reached their climax in a group of pictures of clowns whose torsos and legs are composed of circus figures, animals and stage properties such as drums, batons and jugglers' objects. The *Blue Clown* makes clear how dominant a part metamorphic or double-identity forms had begun to play in Tchelitchew's work. It is interesting that he should have first used these forms in 1929, several years after Max Ernst's revival of them, but in the very year when Salvador Dali began to paint pictures in which metamorphosis and *trompe l'oeil* played a major role. There is little question, however, that Tchelitchew and Dali arrived at their respective enthusiasms for double imagery in complete independence—Dali in Barcelona and Tchelitchew in Paris. Both showed remarkable imaginative gifts in revitalizing a pictorial device of which sixteenth-century precursors like Arcimboldo were fond."—adapted from (6) *Tchelitchew*

Madame Bonjean (opposite). "Since 1929 Tchelitchew had been making drawings of a woman spectator at the circus and in 1930 he achieved a taut and expressive portrait of Mme Jacques Bonjean. He now undertook the difficult task of relating a three-quarter length figure of the same subject to supplementary circus figures projected into space. Here he was aided by that control of line which not even his most persistent detractors were able to deny and by a mastery of atmospheric effect which may one day be recognized as one of his most personal contributions to contemporary art. The figures are inexorably fixed in depth by a strengthening of contour in the handling of the acrobats as opposed to that of Mme Bonjean. The narrow and arbitrary color scale is made to reinforce the linear illusion of a separate spatial existence for each figure, while at the same time acting as a cohesive agent for the over-all composition. . . ."—adapted from (6) *Tchelitchew*

TCHELITCHEW. *Madame Bonjean*. 1931. Oil on canvas, 51¼ x 38¼″. Purchased 1938.